Letter to Parents

Today's world is more complex than ever, with studies revealing that we're navigating an unprecedented number of decisions each day. The digital era has brought an incredible array of tools, information, and resources right to our fingertips, but with it comes an overwhelming abundance of options, often leaving us feeling paralyzed or uncertain about the right path to take. This book, "Money Migration," is here to serve as your guide— providing you with financial and life skills that you can establish and build upon to maximize your effectiveness – and we use these in our own family.

We'll cut through the noise, presenting simple and practical step-by-step approaches tailored to each stage of your child's progress. Whether they're just starting to form habits or preparing to take on the responsibilities of adulthood, we'll equip you and your children with actionable strategies to navigate life's complexities confidently.

Beyond the realm of finances, this journey is about fostering essential life skills and habits that lead to lifelong success. From cultivating resilience and a growth mindset to mastering time management and goal setting, these principles are designed to empower your children to thrive in every aspect of their lives. Together, we'll delve into the practices and mindsets that not only pave the way for personal achievement but also nurture the character and values needed to make a positive impact on the world.

Now is the perfect time to chart a course for success—a blueprint for a future filled with promise, purpose, and possibility. By taking these steps today, you'll be laying the foundation for your children to realize their potential as innovators, leaders, and agents of change. Let's work together to position them as world-changers and history-makers, prepared to leave an indelible mark on the world!

Thanks for allowing me to take this journey with you,

Jason Arnold

Founder, Save the Greenbacks

Table of Contents

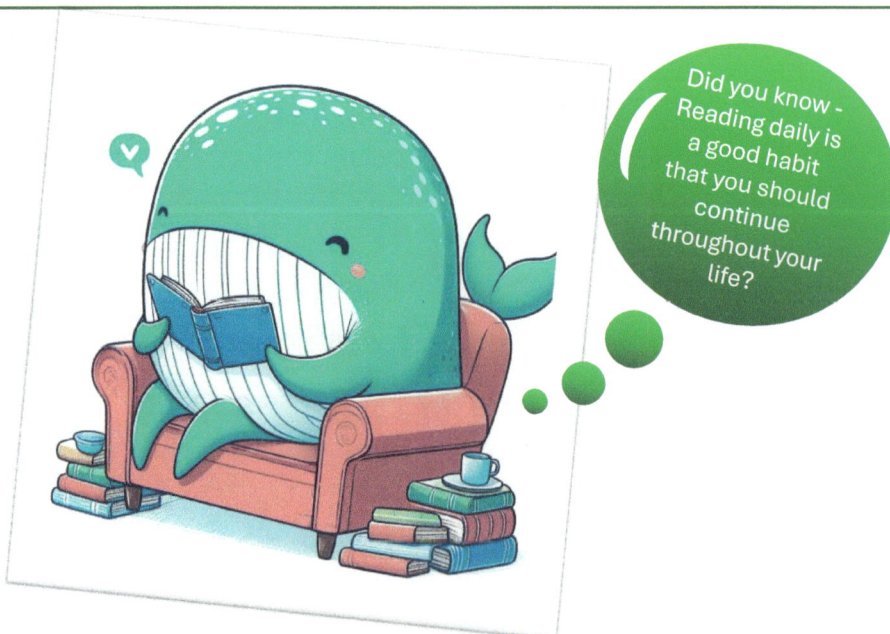

Did you know - Reading daily is a good habit that you should continue throughout your life?

Why read this book? 🫨
Well, we got problems…

- Financial literacy is a fancy term for being good with personal money skills, like spending wisely, saving, and investing.

- Here are common problems of not managing your money well:
    - Overpaying for stuff
    - Borrowing more money to pay bills (that must be paid back)
    - Getting less return on your money
    - Not spotting great opportunities - "a day late and a dollar short"
    - Carrying more stress
    - More likely to be scammed
    - Not achieving dreams and goals

Did you know – almost 90% of **adults** in the US wish they had learned more about managing money in school?

- Many Americans struggle with managing money well – which leads to less money saved. Instead, your money goes to others to pay off debts (we'll talk about this more later). This keeps you from growing your own money to have the life you want!

You can become a Money Genius!

Here's what happens when you're good at managing money…

- **"The more you learn, the more you earn." -Frank Clark**

- **Wait – I'm still in school; why should I get good at managing money at my age?**

  - I'm glad you asked – can you imagine what you can accomplish if you put every dollar you own to work…for you? Think about how that dollar will grow into one, two, three or even more dollars in time. What can you do with that money in the future? By learning these skills now, you can buy that big item you've had your eye on, or go to the movies, or buy stuff on vacation, and have fun!

  - Just think – later, when you're older, you can help buy your own car, get a phone, go to college or even help your parents – the possibilities are endless when you're good at managing money!

  - Being good with money means you can enjoy what you love!

- **What will you accomplish by reading this book? You will…**

  - Learn the basics of financial literacy and managing money well

  - Build a foundation of knowledge that will grow as you do

  - Create a Life Plan and a Budget for your money

  - Practice using the skills we discuss to be ready to apply these to your money and life

  - Be able to help friends, family and others by passing on your learnings to them

Let's dive in and get started!

Learn to Manage Money - Like a Whale Migrates

Managing money has a lot in common with a whale migration. It's a carefully planned, purposeful voyage that ensures survival and well-being. Here's how:

1. **Mapping the Route (Creating a Budget)** Just as whales follow well-established migration routes to find food and avoid harsh conditions, managing money begins with a budget. This "map" helps you stay on course toward your financial goals.

2. **Feeding Grounds (Income Sources)** Whales rely on abundant feeding grounds to sustain their energy, just as you depend on income streams like jobs, investments, or side hustles. Diversifying your feeding grounds (income) ensures you're prepared for the future.

3. **Reserves for the Journey (Savings)** Whales build up fat reserves to sustain themselves during long migrations. Similarly, your savings act as a financial cushion, helping you navigate life's uncertainties.

4. **Avoiding Predators (Financial Risks)** Predators, like sharks, pose threats to whales, much like unexpected expenses or bad investments threaten your finances.

5. **Navigating Currents (Adapting to Changes)** Ocean currents can either help or hinder whales. In money management, economic trends, inflation, or interest rates are similar forces.

6. **Teaching the Pod (Knowledge Sharing)** Whales travel in pods, sharing experiences for collective success. Sharing financial knowledge and discussing strategies with family or mentors helps everyone in your "pod" thrive.

Like a wise whale embarking on its migration, you too can navigate your financial journey with foresight, resilience, and purpose.

Did you know - A baby whale may take up to 15 years to be fully grown!?

*This is **Greenspan**, who we call "**Greeny**" for short – he'll be our guide as we navigate our money journey and will share useful tidbits as we go along.*

What is Money, Anyway?

What's in a Name (of Money)?

Money is known by a lot of different words? Why? Well, we talk about money a lot, and who wants to use the same old word all the time?

Did you know - American money has over 100 nicknames?

Dough: Likely evolved from use of bread, used as early as 1800's

Bucks: Early American colonists traded deerskins, or buckskins

Benjamins: A reference to the one-hundred-dollar bill, like discovering a rare and valuable pearl in the depths of the ocean.

Moola: No one knows its origins, but it's as fun to say as spotting a playful dolphin in the waves!

Cheddar: If someone has the cheddar, it means they've reeled in a big catch of cash

Greenbacks (our favorite): A form of American currency printed during the Civil War, think of a huge green whale

There's a saying, "**Cash is King**" Why do people say that? Because you can get a lot done with money – like buying the stuff you need and giving to people in need.

7

How did money get started in the first place?

- In ancient times, many peoples **bartered** with each other, which is the trading of one object for another

- For example, if I owned a pig, but I needed a chicken for eggs, I could trade my pig to a neighbor who would give me a chicken

- Since a bartering system is inefficient and cumbersome, people desired a more convenient method of buying and selling and eventually introduced early forms of money such as shells and metal for trade

- Money is easier to store, transport and exchange than bartered items

Did you know- The Lydian Lion is among the oldest money ever found?

- Over time, coins became uniform in look and size
- Later, paper money came into existence which is lighter and easier to carry in large amounts
- Most recently, digital money has hit the scene, including cryptocurrencies like Bitcoin and Ethereum

Money just looks like fancy paper –

So, what makes it so special?

If money is just paper, metal, or even digital numbers, why do people get so excited about it? Its value comes from the trust and agreement we all have in it.

- Money serves as a medium of exchange, a unit of account, and a store of value. Since money has a limited supply, there is a demand for it. It's not the physical material of the money that holds worth, but the shared belief in its value and the systems that back it—like governments or central banks.

- Without this shared trust, a $100 bill would be no more valuable than a scrap of paper. This trust allows societies to avoid the challenges of barter, where you'd have to directly trade goods or services, like exchanging pigs for chickens.

- So, money becomes a tool that simplifies trade, builds economies, and represents value efficiently!

Where does our money come from?

- The **Federal Reserve (The Fed)** is the Central Bank of the United States and controls the supply of money.

- The **Bureau of Engraving and Printing** is responsible for printing paper currency.

- The **U.S. Mint** produces coins.

- Federal Reserve notes (bills) are a blend of 25 % linen and 75 % cotton.

- No matter the denomination, a banknote weighs approximately 1 gram. Since there are 454 grams in one pound, this means there are 454 notes in one pound of currency.

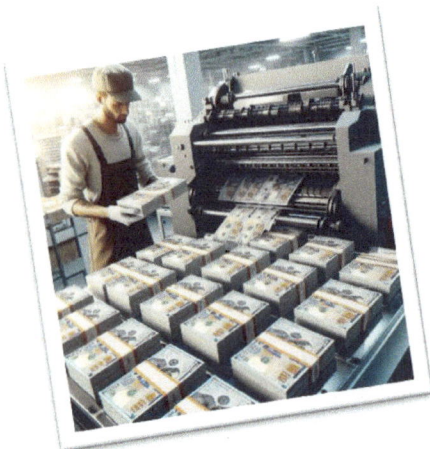

In 1934, the $100,000 Gold Certificate became the highest denomination ever issued. It was never intended for public use but was meant solely for official transactions between Federal Reserve Banks.

Did you know – There is currently over $2 Trillion of US currency in circulation?

The $1 Bill –
What are all those funny symbols?

Letter & number signifies the issuing District of Federal Reserve Bank (12 total Fed Reserve Banks, lettered from A-L) – and occurs frequently on bill

Note Position Number & Letter specifies where on the plate the bill was printed

US Treasury Seal: Used on all paper currency and Treasury documents
- chevron with thirteen stars signifying the original 13 states
- Balance indicates justice
- Key points to authority and trust

Bill Serial Number:
- Each bill has a unique identifying number
- First letter must match issuing Fed Reserve bank
- Number increases sequentially for each bill printed
- Final letter is used to increase possible number of bills in that series

As our first president, George Washington symbolizes independence and democracy

Bill Series: Year listed indicates when this design was applied (not when this bill was printed)

Secretary of the Treasury's signature – a new bill design is implemented each time a new secretary takes office

Did you know- there's a law in place that prohibits the redesign of $1 bill?

Did you know - If a printing error occurs during a press run, a star is added in place of the final letter of a bill's serial number?

Did you know - If the first letter of serial number does not match the Fed Reserve seal letter, the bill is likely counterfeit!?

The $1 Bill –
On the Flip Side

In 1956, President Eisenhower signed into law that the phrase "In God We Trust" be printed on all US paper currency

Three Latin phrases are seen on Great Seal:
- E Pluribus Unum ("Out of many, one")
- Annuit cœptis ("He has favored our undertakings")
- Novus ordo seclorum ("A new order of the ages").

The intricate designs and "webbing" throughout the dollar bill are intended to make counterfeiting (fake copies) of the bill more difficult

The Great Seal (Reverse)
- Unfinished pyramid made of 13 rows of bricks representing the 13 original American colonies
- The Eye of Providence or All-Seeing Eye intends to show God watching over His creation
- Roman numerals on bottom row are "1776," (year the US Declaration of Independence was signed – or America's Birthday!)

Plate number: Front and Back of bill are printed with different plates, so they have different serial numbers

The Great Seal (Obverse)
- The Bald Eagle is a symbol of American Bravery, Freedom & Strength
- Scroll in Beak: Latin phrase indicates that America is made up of many people groups unified under a single government
- Shield on Chest: features 13 stripes and symbolizes resilience
- Olive Branch: symbolizes Peace
- Arrows: symbolizes readiness for war and willingness to defend itself when necessary

Did you know - The Great Seal of the United States is meant to symbolize the ideals of America. First discussed in 1776, it took 5 years to finalize?

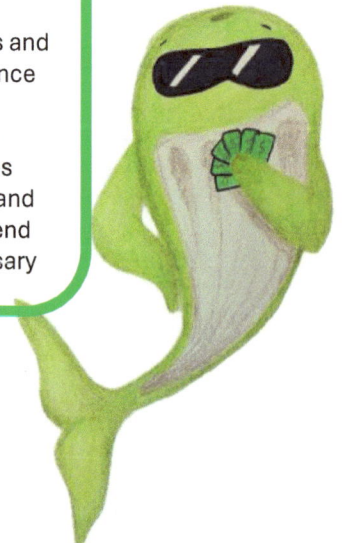

Managing Money

What does a Bank do?

You've probably seen banks all over town where you live, but what goes on there?

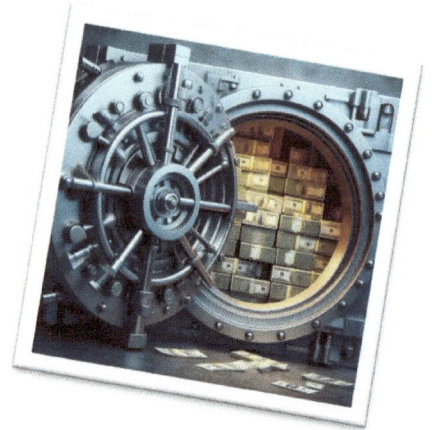

- A bank is a company or business that holds money for their account holders
  - A bank account is a record or statement of financial expenditure and receipts relating to a particular period or purpose
  - Certain bank accounts pay you interest, which is like the bank paying you to rent your money!

- Banks make their own money by lending money to others for homes, cars and credit cards and then collecting interest on these loans

- Banks also have vaults which are large (or small), strong, secure containers or rooms that are designed to protect money from fire, flood, and theft

- What if my bank goes out of business? What happens to my money?
  - The US Government corporation know as FDIC ensures a certain amount of money you have in bank/protects it; if bank fails, you will get this insured portion of your money back!

- Do you think you should bury your money in the backyard, hide it under your mattress or keep it in a bank? Why or Why Not?

Did you know – There are 72,000 commercial bank branches in US?

Overview of Banking Products

- ## What is a checking account?
  - A checking account is a type of bank account where you can make cash withdrawals or deposits (add or remove money). Account owners can use a check register to keep a running balance of their available checking account funds. You can also use a checking account for electronic transfers or purchases, either online or in person. Generally, checking accounts cover everyday expenses, such as rent, utilities, and food.

- ## What is a Debit Card?
  - A debit card is a payment card that deducts money directly from your checking account. Also called "check cards" or "bank cards," debit cards can be used to buy goods or services or to get cash from an ATM.

- ## What is a Credit Card?
  - A credit card is another thin rectangular piece of plastic or metal issued by a bank or financial services company that allows cardholders to borrow funds to pay for goods and services with merchants that accept cards for payment.

- ## What is an ATM used for?
  - An automated teller machine (ATM) is an electronic banking outlet that allows customers to complete basic transactions without the aid of a branch representative or teller.
  - ATMs are convenient, allowing consumers to perform quick self-service transactions such as deposits, cash withdrawals, and transfers between accounts.

Did you know – There are over 400,000 ATM machines in America!?

Modern Money Moving –
We've come a long way from cash and coin...
Digital & Electronic Payments

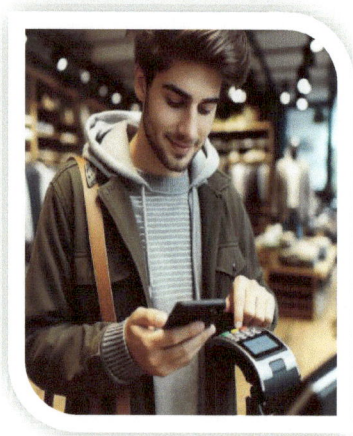

- Credit/Debit Cards: Widely used for online and in-person transactions, offering ease of use and global acceptance. Can often now be contactless where tap-to-pay allows fast and secure payments.

- Mobile Wallets: Apps like Apple Pay, Google Pay, and Samsung Pay allow contactless payments using smartphones or wearables.

- Online Banking: Direct transfers and bill payments through bank websites or apps.

- Peer-to-Peer (P2P) Transfers: Platforms like Venmo, PayPal, and Zelle enable quick money transfers between individuals.

- Cryptocurrencies: Digital currencies like Bitcoin and Ethereum offer decentralized, borderless (not country-specific) transactions.

- QR Code Payments: Scanning QR codes to make payments.

- Buy Now, Pay Later (BNPL): Services like Afterpay and Klarna let users split payments into installments.

What can I do with my money?

There are 4 key uses of money:

Money Action	Purpose
Spend	Buy things for your day-to-day needs, like food, gas for the car, electricity or clothes
Save	Setting aside money for goals like buying a new iPhone or a PlayStation (or a car or house when you're older)
Invest	Putting your money towards higher return (but usually higher risk) ventures such as the stock market, real estate, college saving programs, or a business
Give	Passing your money to a worthy cause, such as feeding the homeless, rescuing puppies, or supporting the arts

spending

saving

investing

giving

- To be most effective with your money, it's best to have a balance of all these activities. Putting too many of your funds towards any of these actions may lead to undesired consequences, so strive for the mix that's best for you as you grow up!

- While money is important, it is simply ONE tool to use as you pursue a full, productive and impactful life!

- Consider: Why is having money considered good? What is your favorite thing to do with money?

Did you know - It's good to save for the future but saving too much can rob you of the joy of living today!

17

Money Mindset: Abundance or Scarcity?

The abundance and scarcity money mindsets represent two contrasting ways of thinking about wealth and resources:

Aspect	Abundance Mindset	Scarcity Mindset
Core Belief	There's enough for everyone.	Resources are limited; there's never enough.
Focus	Growth, opportunities, and long-term success.	Fear, limitations, and short-term survival.
Behavior	Generosity, saving, investing, and calculated risks.	Hoarding, excessive frugality, impulsive spending, or inaction.
Perception of Money	A tool to create opportunities and positive outcomes.	A source of stress, competition, and worry.
Attitude Toward Risks	Open to calculated risks for growth.	Fearful of risks; prefers playing it safe.
Outcome	Financial growth, satisfaction, and opportunities.	Stress, anxiety, and limited financial progress.

These two mindsets significantly influence how individuals handle their finances, make decisions, and perceive opportunities. Shifting from a scarcity to an abundance mindset can lead to healthier money habits and overall well-being. Which of these resonates more with you?

Why is buying stuff so much fun?
The Psychology of Spending

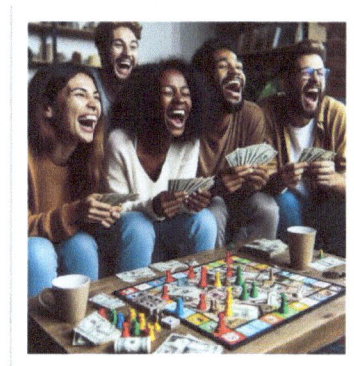

- You've probably heard stories of people who LOVE to spend money on things they WANT and don't know when to stop – this can lead to big problems, like not having money for things we NEED, like food and shelter!

- There's nothing wrong with spending money, but you'll be best set up for the future when balancing spending with the other money actions!

However, spending is probably the most FUN, and here are some reasons for that:

- When you obtain the things you've been longing for, your brain's reward centers light up, increasing neuronal activity and releasing dopamine. As a result, you feel a surge of excitement and happiness, though it only lasts for a short while.

- When we see a deal, we feel that the price of something is less than its true value!

- We think the item will make our life better – we get excited to think about the impact (but this can fade over time).

- A new product can make us look like we fit into a certain crowd and it's a way of being social.

- Making decisions about what to purchase can help us regain a sense of control over our lives.

Did you know - Consumer spending accounts for more than 2/3 of U.S. economic activity?

19

Getting Down to Business...

Make a Life Plan

Let's build a path to success with a step-by-step approach. Remember, your plan is a living document—review and adapt it as your goals and circumstances evolve! We'll plan for success and think like a millionaire!

1. **Start by asking yourself**: What do I enjoy doing? What makes me happy? Make a list of hobbies, activities, or experiences that bring you joy. These will act as a foundation for crafting a fulfilling path forward.

2. **Identify Your Strengths and Resources**: What advantages do you already have? Take stock of your skills, talents, connections, and resources. Recognizing what you already possess can provide clarity and confidence in taking the next steps.

3. **Set Clear Goals and Define your Objectives**: Break these down into categories—short-term (e.g., the next year), medium-term (e.g., 5 years), and long-term (e.g., 10+ years). Write them down to visualize your ambitions.

4. **Explore Life's Possibilities**: Do you want to try new experiences? Do you want to try something outside of your comfort zone? Do you want to see the world? If travel or adventure is on your wish list, include it in your plan and identify opportunities to make it happen.

5. **Assess Costs and Resources Needed**: Financial planning is key. Think through: How much will all this cost? How much will I need? Research expenses related to your goals and create a budget.

Did you know - Those who fail to plan - plan to fail?

6. **Plan for Financial Independence**: If becoming wealthy or achieving financial security is a goal, define steps to reach it. Ask yourself, "If I want to be a millionaire, I need to..." Build your plan to increase income, invest wisely, or start a business that aligns with your passions (more to come on this in the following pages).

7. **Chart Your Path to Success**: With all these pieces in place, create an actionable timeline. Prioritize steps, set deadlines, and celebrate small milestones along the way.

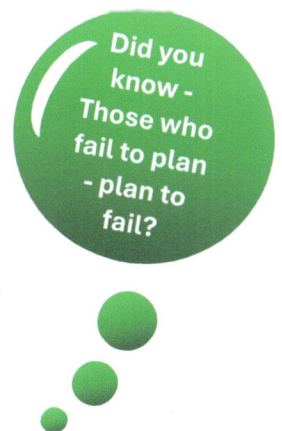

21

How can I make my money last?

- Make a **budget**!...Wait, what's a budget?
    - A budget is **plan** for your money
    - This means you count all your incoming money (allowance, earnings from a job, etc.) and put it toward different categories

- A good starter budget is the 60/30/10 plan:
    - 60% for Spending
    - 30% for Saving
    - 10% for Giving/Tithing

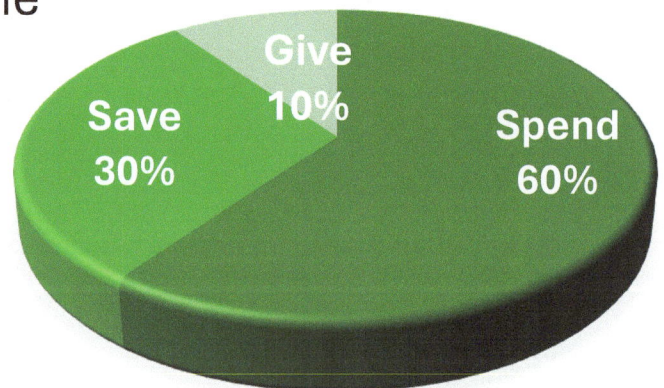

- For example, if you receive $10, you could spend $6 right away, save $3 for the future and give the final $1 to someone in need

- Play around with the percentages to find out what works for you

- These percentages may also change in different stages of life

Did you know – People with a budget are better prepared for emergencies and have better mental health?

Budget Example

- **Incoming Money = $10**
- Money given to you or that you've earned, including:
  - Allowance
  - Birthday money
  - Cash from a job

- A great way to start with a budget is the 3 jars method using our 60/30/10 plan
- Divide the money you have coming in across our 3 categories like in the examples below:

Jar 1: Spend = $6
Candy, Crafts, Toys, Fun

Jar 2: Save = $3
PS5, iPhone, Car, College, House

Jar 3: Give/Tithe = $1
Give to charities, people in need, the Church

Let's Make our first Budget!

This budget can help you make the most of your money!

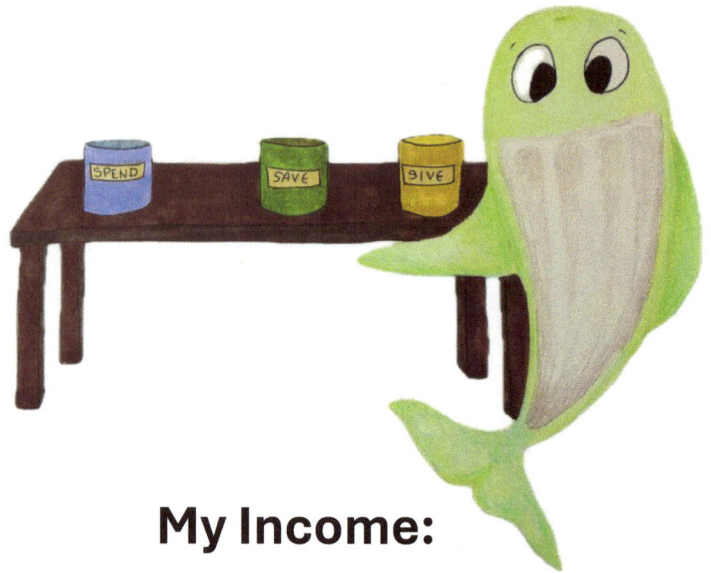

Example Income:

Income	Source
Allowance	$5
Jobs	$15
Other (Birthday Cash)	$20
TOTAL	**$40**

My Income:

Income	Source
Allowance	
Jobs	
Other (_____)	
TOTAL	

Example Budget:

Income Total	$40
Spend (60%)	$24
Save (30%)	$12
Give (10%)	$4

My Budget:

Income Total	
Spend (60%)	
Save (30%)	
Give (10%)	

OK, so I have some money -
How can I make it grow as big as a Whale?

- **Money doesn't grow on trees, but there are ways to help it grow!**

- You've probably heard the term, "**Interest**" before; what does it mean?...in this context, think of interest as you receiving 'rent' from someone else for letting them use your money

- For example, if you have a savings account at a bank, the bank likely pays you regular interest payments because they use your money for their regular operations. You keep the full amount of your money **PLUS** this regular interest payment

Did you know - Albert Einstein said, "The greatest mathematical discovery of all time is compound interest?"

Wait – it gets better! Interest can be compounded!

Compound Interest is when the interest you earn starts earning its own interest!

As you can imagine, compound interest has a snowball effect and continues to get bigger over time, with you getting continually larger interest payments!

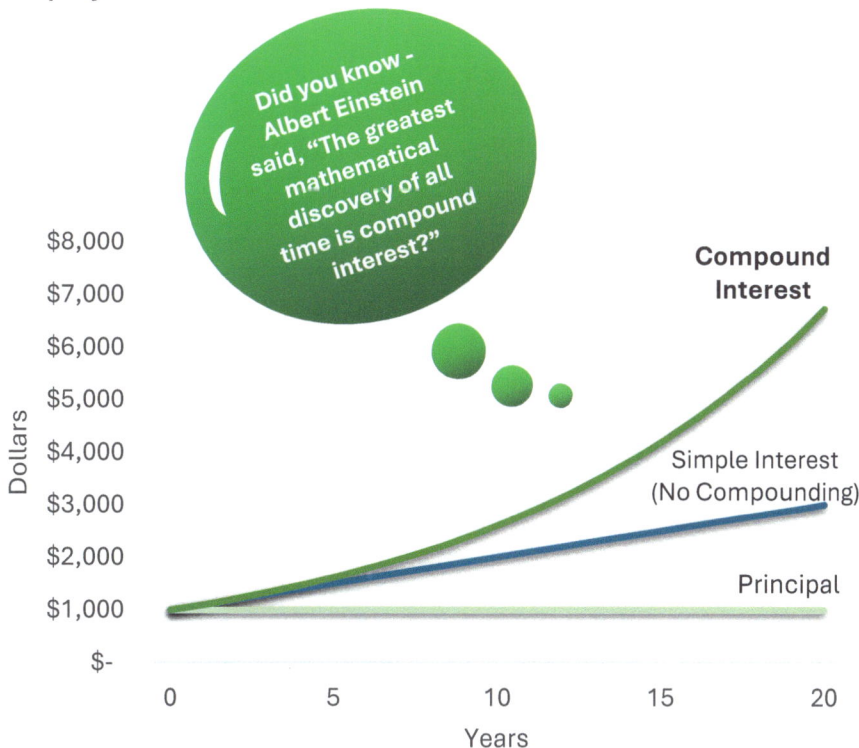

Dollars

$8,000
$7,000
$6,000
$5,000
$4,000
$3,000
$2,000
$1,000
$-

0   5   10   15   20

Years

Compound Interest

Simple Interest (No Compounding)

Principal

25

Money for the Ages

Steps to Take as You Grow Up

Let's build a plan of what to do with money as you age!

Here's an example timeline - adapt as needed for your timing and situation:

Did you know - People who start learning about money at a young age are more likely to achieve greater independence and options as they get older?

Ages 3 – 5: Introduction to Money

Ages 11 – 13: Budgeting Basics

Ages 18+ Financial Independence

Time

Ages 6 – 10: Earning & Saving

Ages 14 – 18: Advancing Financial Skills

Did you miss one or more of these along the way? Don't worry, you can always set these up when it makes sense for you and your family!

Let's dive in!

Ages 3 – 5: Introduction to Money

- Goals:
  - Learn to use money by enjoying games using play money
  - See adults purchasing items at the store with money

- Potential actions to take and examples:
  - Play 'store' using a toy cash register and play games that involve money concepts
  - Receive money as a gift (for birthdays or holidays)
  - Collect lost coins you find
  - Start gathering your spare coins by using a piggy bank
  - Parents/Grandparents could start a savings account at a bank for you (so you start earning compound interest!)

Did you know - Malcom X said, "The future belongs to those who prepare for it today?"

Ages 6 – 10: Earning & Saving

- Goals:
  - Learn more about how money works and its purposes by actively using it to buy things
  - Discover why you don't want to spend every dollar you get immediately
  - Understand that money is earned through working
- Potential actions to take and examples:
  - Collect allowance for doing chores around the house or reading books
  - Set up a neighborhood lemonade stand to learn about financial transactions
  - Sell old toys at consignment shops, yard sales or online (with help of a parent) to gather money for your next purchase
  - Get a wallet or purse to store your "Spend" money when you go out
  - Learn to compare prices and find good deals at the store
  - Identify a more expensive item that you want and begin saving towards that goal

Ages 11 – 13: Budgeting Basics

- Goals:
  - Learn the concept of using money for Needs versus Wants
  - Practice smart spending
- Potential actions to take and examples:

  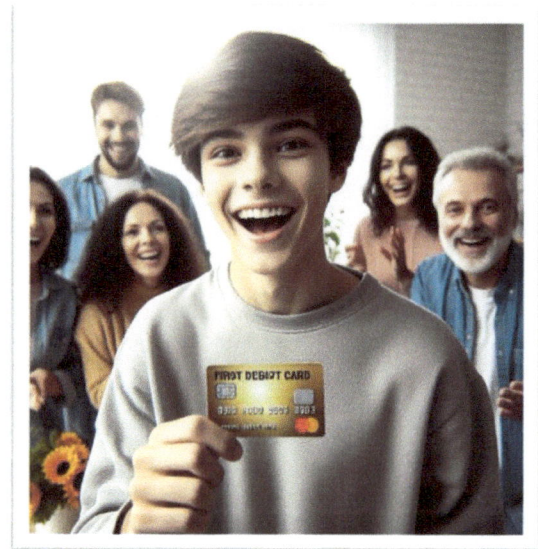

  - Consider your long-term needs or wants (like getting the latest phone), then think about how much money it will take to buy that
  - Become familiar with online banking and paying bills digitally by observing a parent
  - Establish more consistent streams of income
  - Begin the 3 Jar method of categorizing money:
    - Spend, Save, & Give
  - Make your first budget – this can be simple, like Needs versus Wants
    - Needs: Books, Clothes, Shoes
    - Wants: Candy, Toys, Video Games
  - Sign up for your own checking account and debit card with the aid of a parent and begin to use with their support
  - Identify activities or jobs you can do in your area to help neighbors and make some extra money

Ages 14 – 18: Advancing Financial Skills

• Goals:

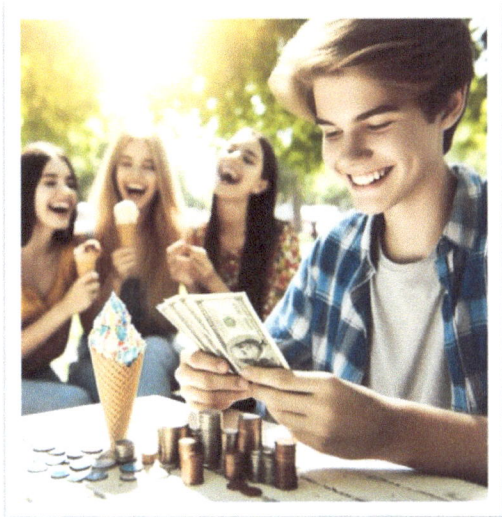

- Establish a more sophisticated budget to address your current needs with additional categories (like costs from having a part-time job, such as gas for driving to work)
- Increase online banking and money management skills, like transferring money
- Understand credit and debt (borrowing money from a bank that you must pay back, with interest)
- Grow knowledge of investing with long-term money growth tools
- Observe how you pay taxes through deductions from your paychecks at a job

• Potential actions to take and examples:

- Discuss with your parents the possibility of them giving you a set amount of money for school clothes and supplies that you are then responsible for purchasing with their oversight
- Use the bank's app where you set up your checking account to monitor your account balance
- Talk to your parents about how they use their credit cards and who they pay for mortgage and car payments
- Get an official job with regular pay (local restaurant, retail, landscaper)
- Set up a brokerage account where you could begin trading high-quality exchange-trade funds (ETFs) in a custodial UTMA (Uniform Transfers to Minors Act) account with your parents' help
- Use your savings account to begin regularly saving money towards a large purchase (such as a car or contributions towards college)

Age 18+ Financial Independence

- Goals:
  - Update your Life Plan to include goals throughout your adult life
  - Maximize your cash flow so you spend less money than you bring in
  - Minimize your debt so you are not paying lots of interest to the bank on credit cards, your house or your car
  - Diversify investments to ensure that your money is consistently growing through the ups and downs of the economy
  - Automate bill payment so you don't miss a due date and have to pay late fees
  - Put every dollar to work!

- Potential actions to take and examples:
  - Launch a full budget with categories tailored to your unique spending, including Rent, Groceries, Insurance, Utilities, Entertainment, Saving, & Giving
  - Build an Emergency Fund – save monthly in a separate bank account until you reach an amount that covers 3-6 months of living expenses to support you in the event of a job loss or other financial emergency
  - Remember the "Auto's": Autosave, Autopay, Auto-invest (more on this coming up)
  - Investigate modern tools available to speed your transactions, including online bill payments and digital networks (like Venmo and Zelle)
  - Establish a retirement plan, and find out what tools are available to you such as a 401(K) plan through your employer, or an Individual Retirement Account (IRA) that provide incentives for long-term savings that you can tap into later in life

Best Practices

Get to Know the Autos...

Did you know – if you automate your routine tasks, you'll have more time to do the things you love!?

There are several ways you can 'automate' your money moves both now and as you grow. Why? After you set these, you can (mostly) forget these! Check this out:

- **Auto-Save**
  - Set up a recurring, automatic transfer from your checking account (usually earning no interest) to a savings account (often earning some interest)
  - Reduces temptations of spending every dollar you have because the money automatically moves to other accounts

- **Auto-Invest**
  - Dollar-cost averaging occurs when you automatically buy investments on a fixed schedule, potentially reducing cost per unit over time
  - Goal achievement can be realized since many investments grow over time, not a lot all at once

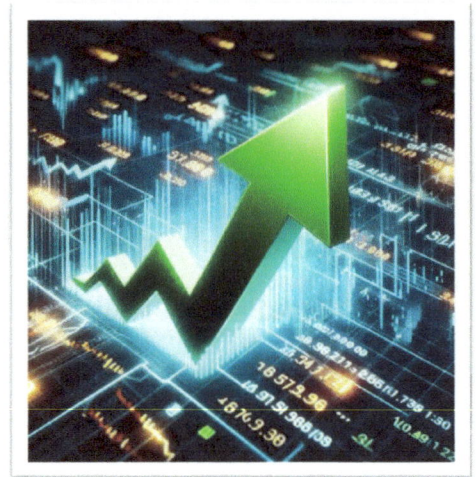

- **Auto-Pay**
  - Avoid late fees by automatically paying bills on time
  - Reduces need for paper bills and checks to be sent in the mail, thus cutting waste

You will be amazed at the impact that automating your financial moves will have – you won't even miss the money, but it can grow substantially to be ready for when you need it, giving you more time to spend with family, friends, or working on your other goals!

How do I make more money as I get older?

- There has never been another time in history with so many ways to make money!

- As the saying goes, **"if you love what you do, you'll never work a day in your life!"**

- So, as you think about what you want to do when you grow up, ask yourself:
  - What do I love to do?
  - What things have I done that others have told me I'm good at?

- Start with your passions – think about what you like to do and what you're good at – these might be different things!

- Think about how these interest areas could turn into ways to earn money

If you love to...	A job could be.....
Make art	Artisan, Craft Designer
Read	Librarian
Work out at the gym	Personal Trainer
Play video games	Programmer
Shop	Personal Shopper
Love to swim	Lifeguard
Help kids	Summer Camp Counselor
Plan a party	Project Manager
Manage money	Financial Planner
Explain things	Teacher
Help people feel their best	Healthcare Field
Play with LEGO's or build stuff	Construction Work
Create something new	Business Owner

Be Your Own Boss!
Business Ideas by Age...

Age 6 – 10
- Lemonade Stand
- Sell baked goods
- Sell stuff in Garage sales

Age 11 – 13
- Dog Sitting/Walking
- Help older people in your neighborhood
- Shovel snow/Rake Leaves
- Sell stuff online

Age 14 – 18
- Babysitting
- Lawn/Landscaping Service
- Online/Tech gigs (help other folks ☺)
- YouTube
- Graphic Design

As you wrap up your time at home and become an adult, you have several options available to you – including work, college, military, starting a business, seeing the world, volunteering, and more!

Did you know - Tony Hsieh said, "Chase the vision, not the money, - the money will end up following you?"

Time – and how to use to your advantage

- When you're young, you have a tremendous resource already available that you might not be thinking of – it's your time!

- The time available to you gives you incredible POTENTIAL! This means that the sky is the limit – you can achieve anything you set your mind to!

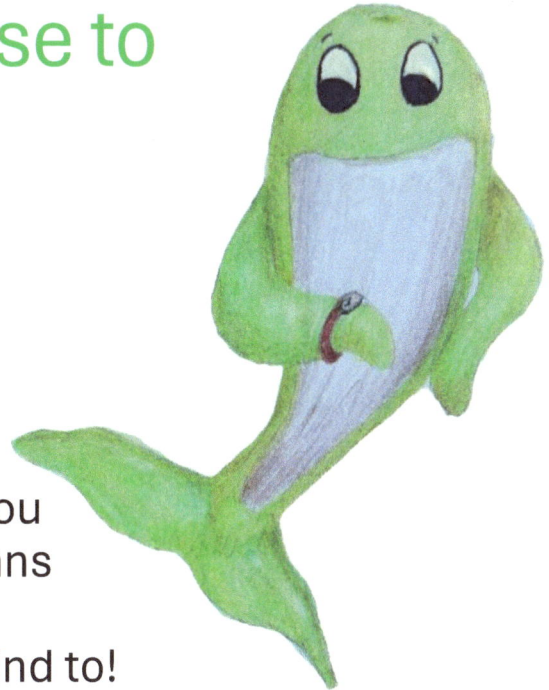

- The time you have can help you in many ways:

  - Time to develop new skills and abilities
  - Time to build your network of people and contacts who can help you
  - Time for your money to grow (compound interest ☺)
  - Time to be a world changer and history maker

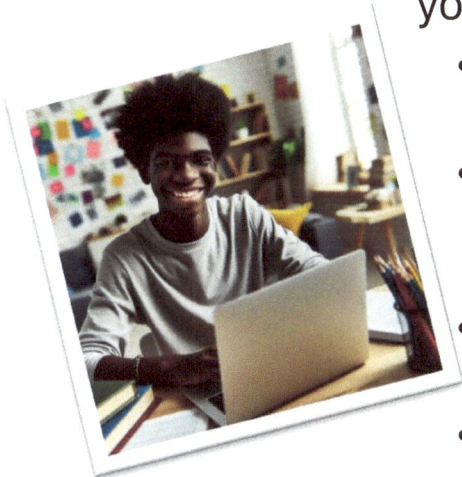

Did you know - Ben Franklin said, "Do you love life? Then do not squander time, for that's the stuff life is made of?"

- As people get older, they don't have as much time to work with, so start while you are young! Make a plan for your life to be successful and help others – you will be amazed at the impact you can have!

Beware!
Protect your money from these Invaders!

Invader	Tell me more...	How you can fight it...
Account Fees	Bank account fees are charges for various services like maintenance, overdrafts, and out-of-network ATM usage	Fees can often be avoided by meeting certain account conditions, including maintaining a minimum account balance or setting up direct deposits
Debt/ Borrowing Costs	When you take out a loan to buy a car, house, or borrow money from a bank using a credit card, you'll be charged interest for these purchases	Buy items with cash when possible so you won't have to open a new loan Pay off credit cards monthly Shop around for loans to find the best interest rate
Inflation	The cost of things you buy often goes up over time – this comes partly from the cost of production increasing	Use a portion of your incoming money to invest in assets that appreciate more like stocks, mutual funds or real estate, so your money is more likely to grow at a rate higher than the inflation rate
Taxes	The federal (national), state and local government will collect a share of your income to pay for things that benefit everyone, like roads, libraries, schools and the military	Identify ways to reduce your tax impact by giving to charity or using legal tools that allow you to utilize tax credits and deductions. Use retirement accounts that provide tax benefits
Fraud	Bad guys will try to trick you to steal your money. This could happen if they call you and tell you that they are from your bank and need your banking password or they might hack into your bank account online Identity theft occurs when someone unlawfully uses another person's personal information, like Social Security numbers or credit card details	Never share your passwords with anyone! If you suspect some problem with your accounts, call your bank directly and ask then if they see anything going on Did you know - There are safeguards you can implement to protect your money?
"Keeping up with the Joneses"	The act of comparing oneself to neighbors, peers, or others around you and striving to match or surpass their lifestyle, possessions, or social status, often to maintain a sense of belonging	Be content with what you have, but never with yourself!

A Sea of Assets

- You've probably heard people talk about other tools for making or growing money – what do you need to know?

- Here are other popular assets right now, with benefits and drawbacks of each

Asset	Examples	Pro's	Con's
Stocks	Stock, mutual funds, ETF's (Exchange-Traded Funds)	Invest your money (and become an owner) in high quality, very stable businesses, some make regular payment back to you (dividends) Historically has grown over time	Depending on several factors, eg data, news, industry news, job reports, value can decrease, and you could lose your entire investment
Bonds	Treasury bonds, corporate bonds	Loan money to the US Federal government, State/Local governments or even corporations (companies) who will then pay you regular interest	Your rate of return from bond interest payments is usually lower than historical stock returns; The debtor could default (not be able to make the required interest payment to you) although this has never happened to US Government
Gold, Silver, and Collectibles	Gold/silver coins/bars, art, wine, stamps, baseball cards, gaming cards, LEGO's (could be almost anything!)	By choosing a collectible that you enjoy, you can have a lot of fun building a collection of sought-after items Returns may not be correlated with stock market, providing a hedge if the market drops	Collectible items value may fluctuate widely or not increase at all. It is hard to predict what a collectible will be worth over time
Real Estate	Houses, fields, apartment buildings, businesses, REIT's (Real Estate Investment Trusts)	Mark Twain said, "Buy land, they don't make it anymore" – there is a limited supply of physical property, making it a finite asset You can live in a property, rent it out, flip a house, or sell it for higher than you bought it for	Often, you will have to obtain a loan from a bank to purchase property, which comes with interest payment and other fees Property values can fluctuate, so you may have to hold onto property for a long time waiting to sell You will pay property taxes on your real estate investment
Crypto-Currencies	Bitcoin, Ethereum, Doge, many others	Cryptocurrencies are digital assets, most often based on blockchain technology (large network of computers) - benefits include cheaper and faster money transfers and decentralized systems that do not collapse at a single point of failure	As a younger asset, there is uncertainty about how cryptocurrencies will be used and their long-term value. They may skyrocket...or be worth nothing at all... Bad guys might try to take advantage of cryptocurrency owners and try to scam them out of their holdings by stealing personal information

Keep Things Simple...

- It's been said you should **"be content with what you have, but never with yourself."**

- There are lots of complicated ways to do things. More complex does not mean better. Generally, when you are first starting out, a simple approach is best.

- Minimize the number of accounts you have; checking & savings accounts are a good place to start. After mastering the use of these accounts, you can then add other accounts in singular fashion.

- A brokerage account will help you invest in stocks, mutual funds and ETFs. The stock market has historically grown at faster rates than inflation

- Later, you can add other accounts if needed. When you are older, your employer may offer a 401(k) account or even a pension.

- Keep it simple and easy to manage – don't open a bunch of new accounts all at once!

Tell me more about the stock market

- Ownership in the overall stock market has traditionally been a good long-term investment as gains in value have generally outpaced inflation.
- The stock market allows companies to raise capital by issuing shares of stock to the public. It also provides investors with opportunities to grow their wealth by benefiting from price appreciation or dividends.
- When you buy a share of stock in a company, you become one of that company's owners.
- If you choose to invest your money in the stock market (buy shares of stock), use money that you won't need for a long time.
- A buy-and-hold investment strategy is a long-term approach to investing where an investor purchases stocks, bonds, or other assets and holds onto them for an extended period, regardless of short-term market fluctuations to take advantage of compounding returns and possibly lower investment fees.
- Investors place orders to buy or sell stocks through brokers. These orders are processed on stock exchanges, where buyers and sellers are matched. Once a trade is executed, ownership of the stock is transferred, and the transaction is settled.
- While investing in the stock market can lead to significant financial gains, it also carries risks due to market volatility, economic changes, and company performance - so talk to a financial planner to find the best strategy for you.
- The stock market can be in a period of growth or decline – here's an overview:

Market Type	Stock Prices Trend	Investor Sentiment	Economic Indicator
Bull Market 🐂	Increasing	Optimistic	Strong growth
Bear Market 🐻	Decreasing	Pessimistic	Weaker economy

You can be an owner of these companies!

Ticker	Company	What they do
AAPL	Apple	Designs and sells electronics like iPhones, Macs, and software services
AMZN	Amazon	Operates e-commerce, cloud computing, and media streaming platforms
CHWY	Chewy.com	Online retail of pet food, supplies, and health products
DIS	Disney	Entertainment, theme parks, and media production
FNKO	Funko	Pop culture collectibles and merchandise
GME	GameStop	Video game and electronics retail
HAS	Hasbro	Toys, games, and entertainment content
HSY	Hershey	Chocolate and confectionery products
KO	Coca-Cola	Produces and distributes soft drinks and beverages worldwide
MAT	Mattel	Toys and dolls like Barbie and Hot Wheels
MCD	McDonalds	Fast food and global restaurant chains
NFLX	Netflix	Streaming movies, TV shows, and original content
RBLX	Roblox	Online gaming and user-generated virtual experiences
TGT	Target	Retail for apparel, home goods, and essentials
TSLA	Tesla	Focuses on electric vehicles, batteries, and clean energy solutions
WMT	Walmart	Retail and e-commerce for everyday goods

Go to **savethegreenbacks.com** for a larger list of stocks from familiar companies!

Thinking about the Future

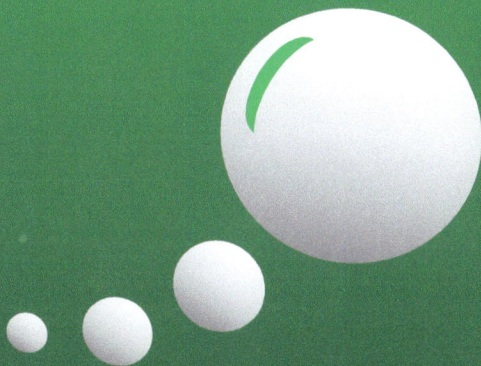

Approaching High School Graduation – What's Next?

- You're nearly there! After years of studying and hard work, you will soon receive your diploma, and the world is at your finger-tips! As you approach this important milestone, leverage your Life Plan to achieve your dreams. Pathways include going to college, directly joining the workforce, signing up for military service, and starting a business.
- Here's a comparison of the most common options:

Aspect	College Path	Non-College Path
Cost	Tuition, fees, and living expenses can add up significantly, potentially leading to student loans.	Generally lower costs but may include vocational training or certifications.
Time Commitment	Typically takes 4+ years to earn a degree.	Can start working right away or complete short-term training programs.
Career Opportunities	Often leads to higher-paying jobs in specialized fields requiring degrees (e.g., medicine, engineering).	Offers quicker entry into trades, entrepreneurship, or creative industries.
Skills Development	Builds academic, professional, and social skills, with access to internships.	Focuses on hands-on experience, practical skills, and on-the-job learning.
Earnings Potential	Degree holders generally have higher lifetime earnings on average.	Non-degree paths can be lucrative, especially in skilled trades or business ownership.
Flexibility	Structured schedules and programs.	Offers more freedom to explore different careers or start a business.
Risk	Risk of accumulating debt without a degree leading to a lucrative career.	Risk of fewer career options in fields requiring formal education.

Each path has its advantages depending on personal goals, interests, and financial situations. Some people even blend the two by pursuing college later in life or combining work with part-time study.

College Path – Common Career Opportunities

- **Healthcare**: Jobs include being a nurse, doctor, pharmacist, physical therapist, or medical researcher.

- **Technology**: Software developer, data analyst, IT manager, cybersecurity specialist, or systems engineer are in-demand roles for tech-savvy graduates.

- **Education**: Teacher, professor, school counselor, or educational administrator for those passionate about learning and teaching.

- **Business and Finance**: Accountant, financial analyst, marketing manager, human resources specialist, or management consultant offer opportunities in corporate environments.

- **Engineering**: Roles like mechanical engineer, civil engineer, aerospace engineer, or environmental engineer are ideal for those with STEM degrees.

- **Law**: Lawyer, legal analyst, compliance officer, or paralegal (though law school may be needed for some roles).

- **Creative Fields**: Graphic designer, architect, writer, editor, or advertising manager for those with creative degrees.

- **Public Sector**: Government positions such as urban planner, policy analyst, diplomat, or social worker can align with degrees in political science, or sociology.

- **Science and Research**: Careers in environmental science, biotechnology, chemistry, or physics for those inclined toward research and innovation.

- **Communication and Media**: Journalist, public relations specialist, content manager, or social media strategist for degrees in communication or media studies.

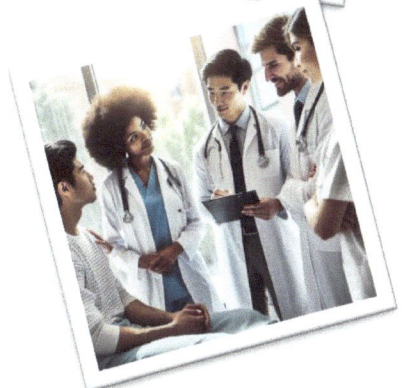

Non-College Path – Common Career Opportunities

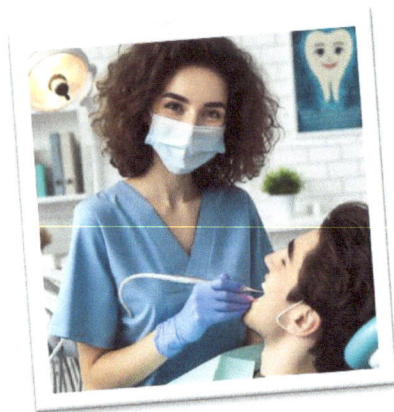

- **Skilled Trades:** Electrician, plumber, welder, HVAC technician, or mechanic. These roles often require vocational training or apprenticeships and are in high demand.

- **Technology:** IT support specialist, software developer (self-taught or through coding bootcamps), or web designer. These roles emphasize skills over formal education.

- **Healthcare:** Dental assistant, medical coder, phlebotomist, or emergency medical technician (EMT). Many healthcare roles require certifications instead of degrees.

- **Sales:** Real estate agent, retail sales supervisor, or sales representative. Success here often depends on interpersonal skills and ambition.

- **Entrepreneurship:** Start your own business, whether it's in landscaping, cleaning services, photography, or e-commerce.

- **Logistics:** Truck driver, delivery driver, or warehouse manager. Certifications like a commercial driver's license (CDL) might be needed.

- **Creative Fields:** Graphic designer, photographer, content creator, or freelance writer.

- **Customer Service:** Hotel manager, call center representative, or retail manager. Climbing the ranks is possible with experience.

- **Construction:** Carpenter, construction laborer, or equipment operator. Practical skills are essential for these well-paying roles.

- **Security and Law Enforcement:** Security guard, police officer, or firefighter. Some positions require academy training.

Life's Best Skills & Habits

As you continue to become savvier with money and are contemplating your path for the future, here are life-long skills you should work on for continued success:

Did you know – Aristotle said, "Excellence is not an act, but a habit?"

1. **Stay Curious** - Embrace a mindset of continuous learning and exploration. Read books, ask questions, seek mentorship, and challenge yourself to grow.

2. **Build your Personal Branding** - Define your unique value—understand what sets you apart from others.

3. **Invest in Yourself** - Take courses to enhance your skills and expand your knowledge base. Develop good habits, like time management and goal setting.

4. **Sell Yourself** - Understand your strengths and articulate them with confidence. Practice storytelling to make your message memorable. Be proactive in reaching out to potential employers or collaborators.

5. **Network** - Build genuine relationships by engaging with peers, mentors, and leaders. Attend events, join relevant groups, and participate in discussions.

6. **Write a great Resume** - Tailor your resume to each job opportunity. Highlight relevant experience, skills, and accomplishments.

7. **Interview well** - Research the company and role thoroughly. Practice answering common questions and prepare your own. Showcase enthusiasm, professionalism, and your ability to solve problems.

8. **Seek Internships** - Gain hands-on experience and industry insights. - Treat internships as opportunities to learn, contribute, and network. Be proactive and show a strong work ethic.

9. **Learn from Failures** - View setbacks as opportunities for growth and reflection. Identify what went wrong and how to improve in the future. Stay resilient—success often comes from persistence.

10. **Be creative** – Look at every situation as a learning opportunity and ask lots of questions and experiment with new ways of doing things!

Change the World by Giving

Giving, whether through time, resources, or kindness, can offer significant benefits to both the giver and the recipient. Here's an overview:

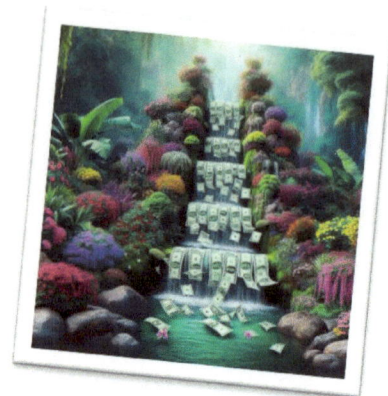

1. **Emotional Well-Being** - Acts of giving can promote happiness and reduce stress by releasing feel-good chemicals like endorphins and oxytocin in the brain.
2. **Stronger Connections** - Giving fosters a sense of community and strengthens relationships, as it often involves supporting others in meaningful ways.
3. **Personal Growth** - Helping others can provide a sense of purpose, build empathy, and boost self-esteem.
4. **Physical Health** - Studies suggest that altruistic behaviors can lower blood pressure and reduce the risk of chronic illnesses.
5. **Positive Ripple Effect** - Generosity is contagious! It inspires others to give, creating a chain reaction of goodwill and impact in communities.
6. **Financial and Professional Rewards** - In some cases, donating to charities can offer tax benefits, and volunteering can lead to new career opportunities and skills.
7. **Cultural and Social Impact** - Giving often addresses societal challenges, improving conditions and opportunities for those in need.

Giving doesn't have to be grand—small, consistent acts of kindness can have a profound impact so, open your wallet and start giving – imagine the impact you can have!

Budget for Time too!

While budgeting your money is extremely important, another area of your life that you should have a budget for is your time.

- As a young person, you may often feel that you have all the time in the world!
- But...as you get older, you will find that you have less time for the things you want to do...
- How do we solve this problem? **Let's apply the budget model to our time!**

Activity	Hours (24 hours/day)
Breakfast	0.5
Get Ready/Drive to School	1
School	7
Sports	1.5
Dinner	1
Family Time/Homework/Hobbies/Reading	4
Sleep	9
TOTAL	**24**

In this example, you could have quality family time, such as a game night, walk/hike, or a conversation!

49

Migration's
End

Your worth is not tied to money!

- At **Save the Greenbacks**, we want you to have a very successful life. Our primary focus is to help you become very good at managing money now so that when you are older, you have developed habits that enable you to lead a fulfilled, impactful life!

- But even more important is for you to know that whatever happens in your life, you have unlimited value and potential. If you never have a lot of money or experience some setback that prohibits you from living out your dreams, you are super special and you have a combo of skills and abilities that no one else has on Earth! Use what you do have to help others and never forget your great worth! We love you and we are rooting for you!

- Imagine yourself in old age – as you think about this future version of yourself, what do you think you will find important? It will likely be that you enjoyed the time you had with friends and family, that you followed your dreams and that you helped others in a way that will carry on after you are gone.

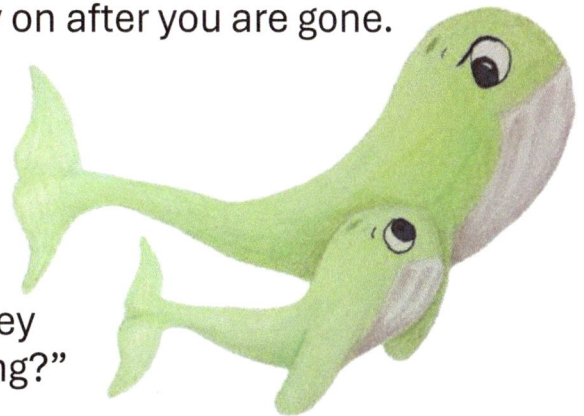

- Ask yourself in life, "If time and money were no object, what would I be doing?"

- **You are worth more than you can ever imagine!**

Congratulations!

You have arrived at your destination and reached the end of your **Money Migration!**

- You are well on your way to being a **Money Genius**
- But learning is a lifelong process, so come back and reread the parts you want to strengthen
- Then put these lessons and habits into practice
- As you master these concepts, you will become more successful and better able to help your family, friends and those in need – nice work!

Pass on what you have learned!

- **Thank you for reading "Money Migration!"**

- By building the skills and habits listed in this book, you will: have a plan for your life and money, be able to follow your dreams, and use your time and resources to make the world a better place!

- As you apply these habits, pass on what you have learned to others. By sharing these new skills, you can create a ripple effect by helping people who help people to achieve the same success!

- Bounce ideas off each other, experiment with new concepts and keep learning - imagine what kind of impact you will have!

SAVE THE GREENBACKS

- For more tools and resources, visit:
savethegreenbacks.com

The **Save the Greenbacks** website is a great resource!

Check back often for new products and ideas!

At Save the Greenbacks, we have a growing catalog of products to help you take your financial knowledge to the next level, including free tools and templates!

Check out **savethegreenbacks.com** today!

Glossary

Term	Definition
Asset	Property of a person, association, corporation, or estate applicable or subject to the payment of debt
Credit	A balance in a person's favor in an account OR a sum placed at a person's disposal by a bank
Debit	Charge against a bank deposit account
Debt	A state of being under obligation to pay or repay someone or something in return for something received, a state of owing
Expense	Financial burden or outlay, a cost
Finance	The system that includes the circulation of money, the granting of credit, the making of investments, and the provision of banking facilities
Financial Literacy (or Acumen)	The ability to understand and effectively use various financial skills, including personal financial management, budgeting, and investing.
Income	A gain or recurrent benefit usually measured in money that derives from capital or labor
Invest	To commit something (like money) in order to earn a financial return
Ledger	Book containing accounts to which debits and credits are posted from books of original entry
Liability	Obligation to pay back an amount that is owed
Migration	A journey of going from where you are to where you want to be

Test your Knowledge!

1. What are some of the common problems people face when they don't manage their money well?

2. How is managing money like a whale migration?

3. Why is it important to learn about managing money at a young age?

4. What are the four different uses of money?

5. Can you explain the concept of compound interest and why it's beneficial?

6. What are some ways to protect your money from "invaders" like account fees and fraud?

7. How can you make a budget using the 60/30/10 plan?

8. How many total whales do you count in this book (including front and back covers)?

References to keep learning!

Check out these books, sites and resources to keep growing your financial expertise!

- **Save the Greenbacks**
  - savethegreenbacks.com
- Books:
  - The 7 Habits of Highly Effective People by Stephen Covey
  - Essentialism: The Disciplined Pursuit of Less by Greg McKeown
  - StrengthsFinder 2.0
- Investopedia.com
  - A plethora of financial content
- References used in this work:
  - Bankrate: "How a lack of financial literacy could be costing you thousands" by Karen Bennett
  - When – and why – did people first start using money? by Chapurukha Kusimba 2017
  - How Stuff Works: "What Do the Symbols on the U.S. $1 Bill Mean?" by Sarah Gleim
  - UScurrency.gov: $1 Note Issued 1963 to Present
  - Kids' Money - How to Explain Banking to Kids
  - Words Matter by Wix: "100 Slang Words for Money and How They Were Coined"
  - Finance Fundamentals: The Four Things You Can Do With Money | Everyday Money with Hannah Moore
  - Why Does Spending Money Feel So Good? by Daniel Kolitz 2020

Did you know – the humpback whale migration is the farthest of all mammals?

About the Author

Jason Arnold is passionate about helping you master your own financial situation so you can enjoy the best that God has for you! Using the principles available from Save the Greenbacks, you can break through the surface financially and live with confidence and security. These same habits enabled Jason to become debt-free and travel the world! Jason has served as a coordinator for the Dave Ramsey Financial Peace University course, has completed the Crown Financial Ministries course, finished Certified Financial Planner (CFP) coursework, and passed the FINRA Security Industry Essentials (SIE), Series 6 and Series 63 exams.

Jason holds a Bachelor of Science degree and an MBA. He lives near Indianapolis, Indiana with his wife and kids.

I would love to hear from you!

Contact Jason at:

jason@savethegreenbacks.com

Disclaimer: This book provides only ideas and does not intend to offer personalized financial advice. For assistance with your personal situation, please consult a licensed financial professional.

www.ingramcontent.com/pod-product-compliance
Lightning Source LLC
Chambersburg PA
CBHW052054190326
41519CB00002BA/216

*9 7 9 8 9 9 9 8 9 1 3 3 0 3 *